LOOKING AT COUNTRIES

Looking at
SPAIN

Jillian Powell

GARETH STEVENS
GS PUBLISHING
A Member of the WRC Media Family of Companies

Please visit our web site at: **www.garethstevens.com**
For a free color catalog describing **Gareth Stevens Publishing's** list
of high-quality books and multimedia programs, call 1-800-542-2595 (USA)
or 1-800-387-3178 (Canada). Gareth Stevens Publishing's fax: (414) 332-3567.

Library of Congress Cataloging-in-Publication Data

Powell, Jillian.
    Looking at Spain / Jillian Powell.
        p. cm. — (Looking at countries)
    Includes index.
    ISBN-13: 978-0-8368-7672-7 (lib. bdg.)
    ISBN-13: 978-0-8368-7679-6 (softcover)
    1. Spain—Juvenile literature. I. Title.
    DP17.P86   2007
    946—dc22   2006034465

This North American edition first published in 2007 by
Gareth Stevens Publishing
A Member of the WRC Media Family of Companies
330 West Olive Street, Suite 100
Milwaukee, Wisconsin 53212 USA

This U.S. edition copyright © 2007 by Gareth Stevens, Inc.
Original edition copyright © 2006 by Franklin Watts.
First published in Great Britain in 2006 by Franklin Watts,
338 Euston Road, London NW1 3BH, United Kingdom.

Series editor: Sarah Peutrill
Art director: Jonathan Hair
Design: Storeybooks Ltd.

Gareth Stevens editor: Dorothy L. Gibbs
Gareth Stevens art direction: Tammy West
Gareth Stevens graphic designer: Charlie Dahl

Photo credits: (t=top, b=bottom, l=left, r=right, c=center)
Jose Aitzelai/AGE: 25b. Paco Ayala/AGE: 12, 22. Bernd Ducke/A1 Pix: front cover, 7, 9, 14, 26b.
Macduff Everton/Image Works/Topfoto: 21tl. Eye Ubiquitous/Hutchison: 4, 19. Paco Gómez García/AGE: 13.
Gunter Gräfenhain/A1 Pix: 18. HAGA/A1 Pix: 10tr, 24. Kneer/A1 Pix: 1, 11. Koserowsky/A1 Pix: 15b. Javier
Larrea/AGE: 15t, 17b. Petra Loewen/A1 Pix: 21cr. Alberto Paredes/AGE: 17t, 23. Prosport/Topfoto: 25t.
Jordi Puig/AGE: 10cl. José Fuste Raga/zefa/Corbis: 27. David Samuel Robbins/Corbis: 20. P. Siegenthaler/
A1 Pix: 6, 8, 16. Superstock: 26t.

Every effort has been made to trace the copyright holders for the photos used in this book. The publisher apologizes,
in advance, for any unintentional omissions and would be pleased to insert the appropriate acknowledgements in any
subsequent edition of this publication.

Printed in Canada

1 2 3 4 5 6 7 8 9 10 10 09 08 07 06

Contents

Words that appear in the glossary are printed in **boldface** type the first time they occur in the text.

Where is Spain?

Spain is in southwestern Europe. It is one of two countries on the Iberian **Peninsula**, which forms the southwestern tip of Europe.

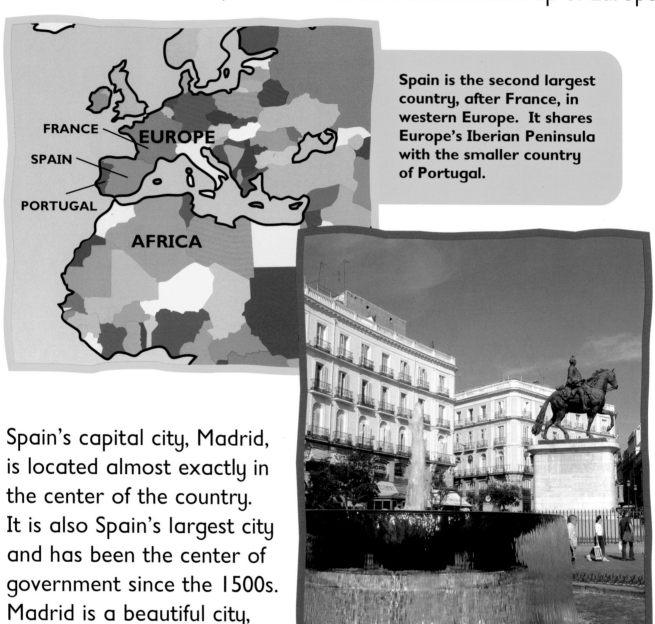

Spain is the second largest country, after France, in western Europe. It shares Europe's Iberian Peninsula with the smaller country of Portugal.

Spain's capital city, Madrid, is located almost exactly in the center of the country. It is also Spain's largest city and has been the center of government since the 1500s. Madrid is a beautiful city, with grand squares, busy avenues, historic buildings, and a world-famous art gallery called the Prado.

Madrid has many squares, or plazas. This plaza is in the center of the city.

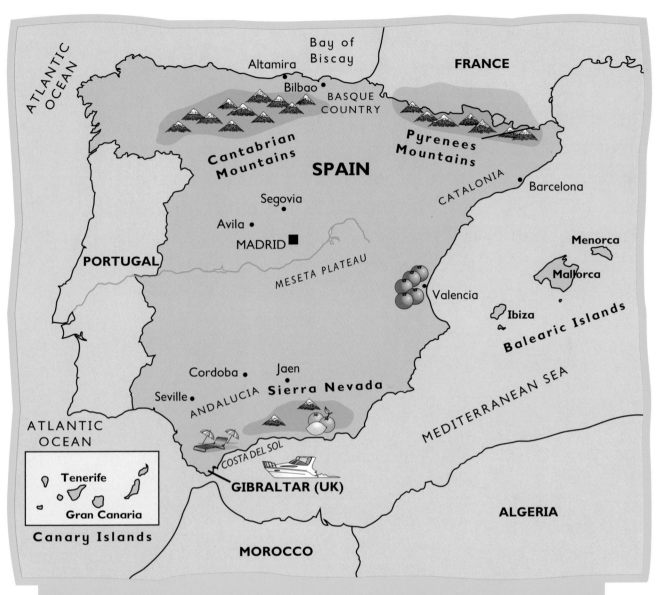

This map shows all the places that are mentioned in this book.

Spain shares land borders with France and Portugal and has a long coastline along three large bodies of water: the Bay of Biscay, the Atlantic Ocean, and the Mediterranean Sea. The Balearic Islands, in the Mediterranean, and the Canary Islands, in the Atlantic, off the coast of West Africa, are part of Spain.

Did you know?

Madrid has the highest **altitude** of any capital city in Europe.

The Landscape

The largest part of Spain's landscape is a high, dry plateau called the **Meseta**. The Meseta covers the entire middle of the country. There are areas of flat farmland both north and south of the plateau. The farmland is dry but **fertile**. The plains along the Mediterranean coast are also fertile farmland. Some areas of Spain's hot, dry south are like deserts.

Meseta means "table." The land on the Meseta is flat, like a table.

The mountains of the Sierra Nevada stand tall in the distance behind the city of Jaen, in the southern region of Andalucia.

Spain also has high mountain ranges. The Pyrenees and the Cantabrian mountains are in the north. The Sierra Nevada is in the south.

Weather and Seasons

On the high Meseta, the weather can be very hot and dry in summer and freezing cold in winter.

South of the Meseta, along the Mediterranean Sea, and on the Balearic Islands, the weather is hot and sunny in summer and mild in winter.

Did you know?

Parts of Spain have sunshine three hundred days a year!

The hot, sunny summers and mild winters of Spain's Costa del Sol make it popular with tourists all year round.

Skiing and other snow sports bring tourists to the Sierra Nevada.

Northern Spain and the mountain areas have more rain and cooler temperatures than other parts of the country. In winter, the Pyrenees and Sierra Nevada mountains have heavy snow.

Sierra Nevada means "snowy mountains" in Spanish.

Spanish People

The Spanish people are proud of their **culture**. They have kept cultural **traditions** such as bullfighting and **flamenco** music and dancing for hundreds of years.

Spanish dancers in Valencia dress in that region's **folk costumes** to celebrate the festival of Saint Joseph.

This woman is lighting a candle at a Roman Catholic cathedral in Barcelona.

Most Spanish people are Roman Catholics, but Spain also has small numbers of Protestants, Jews, and Muslims. Religion is an important part of life in Spain. Even Spanish **fiestas** are almost all religious events.

Did you know?

The caves at Altamira, in northern Spain, have pictures inside them that were painted more than 14,000 years ago.

The people of Mallorca, one of the Balearic Islands, enjoy shopping for fresh, local foods at street markets.

Spain is divided into seventeen regions. The people of each region have their own traditions, folk costumes, and styles of cooking. Some regions, such as Catalonia and Basque Country, have their own flags and languages, too.

School and Family

Most Spanish children start school when they are two or three years old and stay in school until they are at least sixteen.

Like many other children throughout the world, Spanish children often do schoolwork in their school libraries.

The school day usually starts at 8:30 or 9:00 a.m. and lasts until 5:00 p.m. Students have a long lunch break in the middle of the day, which is the hottest time of day.

After school, Spanish children enjoy playing sports or watching television.

Did you know?

Spanish children usually have two last names, one from their mothers and one from their fathers.

When they are not in school, Spanish children enjoy playing games together. These children are playing a game of soccer on the streets of Avila.

Most Spanish families are **close-knit**, and staying close is important to them. Relatives, even in very large families, get together often. Children commonly join adults when families eat out, even when the meal goes late into the evening. In Spain, evenings are a time for walking, window shopping, and meeting friends.

Country Life

Fewer than one-quarter of Spain's people live in countryside areas. Over the years, many younger people have moved away from the countryside to find work in cities and towns.

Most people still living in Spain's countryside either farm the land or raise animals. Cattle are raised mainly in the north, and sheep and goats in the south and on the Balearic Islands.

In central Spain, many people raise sheep, even if they do not own land.

Wheat, barley, and sunflowers are the main crops grown in Spain. In the hot, dry south, farmers also grow almonds, olives, oranges, and lemons.

Spain's warm, dry weather helps crops such as wheat to ripen.

Did you know?

Spain is one of the least crowded countries in Europe.

Almond trees surround this farmhouse on the island of Mallorca.

City Life

Most people in Spain live in or near cities or towns. Many live in the **suburbs** and travel to cities, each day, to work. The largest cities in Spain are the capital city of Madrid and the city of Barcelona, which is in the Catalonia region.

Spain's capital, Madrid, is a historic city, but it is also a lively, modern city with wide avenues and lots of traffic.

Most Spanish cities are built around a main square called the *plaza mayor*. This huge cathedral stands at one corner of the Plaza Mayor in Segovia.

The cities are the richest and busiest places in Spain, with many tourists visiting **inland** cities such as Madrid and Seville as well as coastal cities and island **resorts**.

Did you know?

The plazas in Spanish cities can be round, oval, or rectangular, as well as square.

Public transportation in Spain's cities includes buses, trains, and electric **trams**, like this one from the city of Bilbao.

Spanish Houses

In southern Spain, many of the houses are built from clay or stone. To keep them cool, they have whitewashed walls and small windows, with shutters that can be closed to keep out the heat. Inside, houses often have tiles on the walls and floors, which also helps keep them cool.

Whitewashed walls are common on houses in Cordoba, a city in the southern region of Andalucia. In the cities, older houses like these are on narrow streets.

Several of these apartment buildings in Seville have balconies with glass walls.

Most people in Spain's cities and towns live in blocks of apartment buildings, either right in the city or in nearby suburbs. Some city apartment buildings have shops on the ground floor.

Did you know?

In southern Spain, some people live in cave homes, built into rocky hillsides.

Spanish Food

Many regions of Spain have their own foods and styles of cooking. Many dishes in the north are made with beans. Popular dishes in the east often include rice.

The cities and towns in Spain have many markets where people can buy fresh fish, meat, fruits, and vegetables. Spain also has supermarkets, grocery stores, and small shops such as bakeries.

Spanish markets offer a wide choice of fresh foods. Many of them also have clothes and household goods for sale.

Many Spanish restaurants and cafés have tables for eating outside.

Paella is a favorite Spanish dish. It contains rice, shellfish, meat, peppers, and olives.

Food is an important part of family life in Spain. Spanish people enjoy sitting down together for big midday meals or going out in the evenings to eat at restaurants and cafés. Many cafés serve tapas, which are small plates filled with a variety of snack foods, including sausages, fish, and potatoes.

Did you know?

The Spanish word *paella* means "pan." People usually cook, and share, this popular dish in a large pan.

At Work

Spanish people work in stores, offices, hotels, banks, schools, and factories.

The city of Madrid has many offices and banks. Barcelona and Basque Country are important industrial centers. Spanish factories make cars, machine tools, plastics, and **textiles**. There are also factories that process chemicals or make food or wines.

Many city people in Spain work in offices.

In cities and coastal towns, many people work in the tourist industry. In coastal areas, jobs in farming and fishing are common, too.

Tourism provides jobs in hotels, restaurants, and cafés. This waiter is serving tapas.

More than fifty million tourists visit Spain each year. Tourists buy Spanish crafts, such as pottery, leather goods, jewelry, and rugs.

Having Fun

The people of Spain enjoy colorful fiestas, or festivals. Some fiesta's celebrate religious holy days. Some honor Roman Catholic saints. Others mark seasonal events, such as the harvest, or feature local foods.

The April Fair, in Seville, features colorful flamenco dancers. This annual fiesta attracts visitors from all over the world.

Did you know?

The region of Valencia has a tomato-throwing festival every year at the end of August.

Spanish people celebrate fiestas with music, dancing, and eating. Many fiestas also include noisy street parades and fireworks displays.

Spain is a nation of soccer fans. People flock to soccer games to cheer for well-known Spanish teams such as Réal Madrid.

Soccer, tennis, golf, and cycling are all popular sports in Spain. Some traditional sports have been played in Spain for hundreds of years. They include *pelota*, which is a ball game that is usually played on a walled court, and the spectator sport of bullfighting.

Millions of people play the Spanish **lotteries**. The most famous lottery is El Gordo, which means "the fat one."

Spain: The Facts

- Spain is a **monarchy**. The king is the **head of state**, and a prime minister leads the government.

- The country is divided into seventeen regions. Each region has its own elected government.

- Spain is a member of the European Union.

The euro (left) replaced the old Spanish currency, pesetas (right), in 2002.

The Spanish flag has a wide band of yellow between two narrow red bands. On the yellow band, the national **coat of arms** shows the union of four old kingdoms.

Barcelona is the second biggest city in Spain. About 1.5 million people live there.

- More than forty-four million people live in Spain today, and more than three million of them live in the capital city of Madrid.

Did you know?

Spain has more than ten thousand castles.

Glossary

altitude – the distance or height above sea level

close-knit – having a strong and loving relationship

coat of arms – a special symbol that identifies a particular family or country

culture – the way of living, beliefs, and arts of a nation or a specific group or society of people

fertile – having rich soil that is good for growing crops

fiestas – festivals

flamenco – lively Spanish folk music that usually has a guitar as the main instrument and often includes quick, foot-stamping dance steps

folk costumes – special kinds of clothing that are passed down through generations in a particular country

head of state – the main representative of a country

inland – describing the areas of a country away from any coastlines or large bodies of water

lotteries – games of chance for which people buy tickets and hope their names or numbers will be drawn to win valuable prizes or large amounts of money

Meseta – the high area of flat, dry, almost treeless land that covers most of Spain

monarchy – a country or government that is ruled by a king or a queen

peninsula – a strip of land surrounded by water on three sides

resorts – places, usually on or near lakes or oceans, that have food, lodging, and entertainment for visitors who come there to relax or to spend their vacations

suburbs – areas outside of large cities, made up mostly of homes where people live, instead of places where people work

textiles – threads, yarns, woven materials and cloths, or fabrics

traditions – the ways of living and beliefs of certain people that have been passed down through generations

trams – bus- or trainlike passenger vehicles that run on rails

Find Out More

Castles of the World: Spain
www.castles.org/castles/Europe/Western_Europe/Spain/

Children in Spain
scroggs.chccs.k12.nc.us/~abernad-calhoun/tesoro.htm

DSO Kids: Spanish Culture, Spain
www.dsokids.com/2001/dso.asp?PageID=298

Time for Kids: Spain
www.timeforkids.com/TFK/hh/goplaces/main/
    0,20344,1534234,00.html

Publisher's note to educators and parents: Our editors have carefully reviewed these Web sites to ensure that they are suitable for children. Many Web sites change frequently, however, and we cannot guarantee that a site's future contents will continue to meet our high standards of quality and educational value. Be advised that children should be closely supervised whenever they access the Internet.

My Map of Spain

Photocopy or trace the map on page 31. Then write in the names of the countries, bodies of water, regions, islands and island groups, cities, and land areas and mountains listed below. (Look at the map on page 5 if you need help.)

After you have written in the names of all the places, find some crayons and color the map!

Countries
France
Portugal
Spain

Bodies of Water
Atlantic Ocean
Bay of Biscay
Mediterranean Sea

Regions
Andalucia
Basque Country
Catalonia

Islands and Island Groups
Balearic Islands
Canary Islands
Mallorca

Cities
Altamira
Avila
Barcelona
Bilbao
Cordoba
Jaen
Madrid
Segovia
Seville
Valencia

Land Areas and Mountains
Cantabrian Mountains
Costa del Sol
Meseta Plateau
Pyrenees Mountains
Sierra Nevada

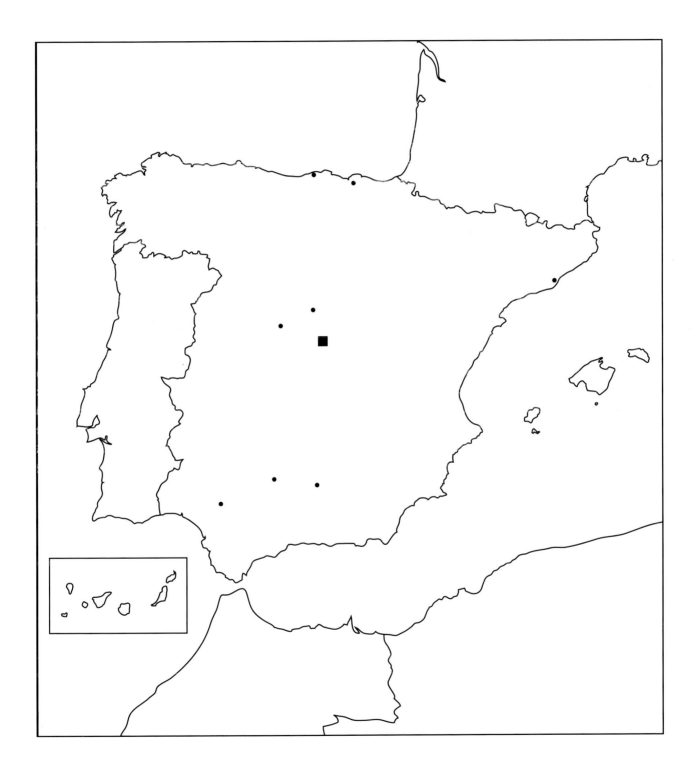

Index